P9-CRK-544

ISAAC FOX LIBRARY

ANIMAL PREY

Zebras

SANDRA MARKLE

⎿ LERNER PUBLICATIONS COMPANY/ MINNEAPOLIS

THE ANIMAL WORLD IS FULL OF
PREY.

Prey are the animals that predators eat. Predators must find, catch, kill, and eat other animals in order to survive. But prey animals aren't always easy to catch or kill. Some have eyes on the sides of their heads to let them see predators coming from all directions. Some are colored to blend in and hide. Some prey are built to run, leap, fly, or swim fast to get away. And still others sting, bite, or use chemicals to keep predators away.

In Africa, zebras live in herds, or groups, that work together to survive. Burchell's zebras migrate (move) across the Serengeti Plain of eastern Africa. Each year they follow the seasonal rains. *Along the way, they are stalked by hungry predators.*

It's a hot, dry day in late June on the Serengeti. The rainy season is over. Each day the grass becomes drier. So the big herd of hundreds of Burchell's zebras slowly moves northward. There, short periods of rain still help the grass grow.

Within the large herd are smaller family units. A family is made up of a single stallion, or male zebra, and three or more mares (females) and their foals (babies). Zebras give birth throughout the year, so the family's youngsters range in age from newborns to two years old. Today, in the early morning light, the newest member of one zebra family is born. It's a little male. His mother quickly grooms him, licking him clean. This helps her learn his smell so she'll be able to pick him out in groups of zebra youngsters.

After baby zebras are born, they can stand and walk within minutes. The new mother nudges the little male to his feet. Then she gently pushes him toward her udder, the milk-filled sac between her hind legs, where he nurses. In less than an hour, he is strong enough to travel with his family.

Every zebra has its own unique scent and pattern of stripes. Using these markers, the baby is able to keep track of his mother.

The zebra families stay close together as they walk on across the plain to their new grazing spot. Each family group forms its own single-file line. The new mother takes her usual place in her family line, and the little male falls in beside her. The stallion sometimes leads, but today he guides his family from the end of the line. He frequently lifts his head to look for predators that might be trying to sneak up on his family.

When the family stops to graze, the stallion stays on guard. With big eyes high on its head, a zebra can watch for predators even while grabbing a mouthful of grass. Zebras' eyes are widely spaced. They can see almost all the way around without turning their heads.

This time, though, it's the stallion's sharp hearing that alerts him to danger. He lifts his head and arches his neck as he focuses on a rustling sound. The mares immediately recognize his warning pose. They lift their heads and turn their ears to listen for any sound from an animal that might be stalking them.

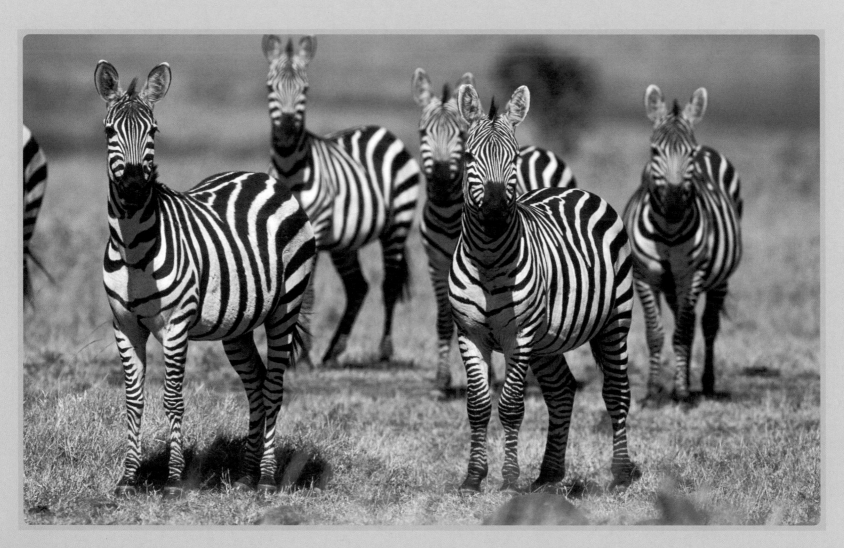

Suddenly, a lioness explodes out of the tall grass. Zebras are quick and agile. The instant they see the hunter, they turn and run. Their sharp-edged hooves help them dig in and kick off the ground in long strides. Their hooves kick dust into the face of the big cat.

Almost instantly all of the zebras join in the stampede. All these moving striped targets can confuse a predator. But the lioness spots a mare that lags behind. In a burst of speed, the lioness closes in on her prey. And as soon as the lioness judges she's close enough, she pounces, digging her strong, sharp claws into the zebra's hindquarters.

The mare's only chance to escape is to use her most powerful defense. She kicks out with both back legs. The zebra's hooves can break bones. This time, the mare only manages a glancing blow to the big cat's chest. Still, it's enough to make the lioness break off the attack.

The stallion charges to the mare's defense, and the lioness lopes off. The wounded mare rejoins her family.

The herd moves on. The hungry little male walks under his mother's neck to stop her. He moves to her back legs, reaches under her belly, and grabs a teat in his mouth. She lets him nurse for a few minutes. Then she walks on, forcing him to trail after her.

Each time the zebra herd stops to graze,
the little male nurses for a few minutes. At midday, when it's hot
and the herd rests, the mare lets her foal nurse again. Then she lies down
in the golden, dry grass to sleep, and he lies down beside her. But the
youngster is too full of energy to rest for very long. Soon he's running,
bucking, and even jumping over his mother's back just for the fun of it.

Zebras have to drink at least once each day. They go for water during daylight hours, when there's a better chance of spotting predators. Rivers are especially dangerous for zebras. Lions and cheetahs may sneak up behind them, and crocodiles lurk in the water. These hunters can swim with only their nostrils and eyes above water. Some of the zebras keep watch onshore, ready to bark an alarm at the first sight of a crocodile. Those drinking in the river stay close together and watch for swimming predators too.

Each year the zebras follow the rains across their range. They like to eat the tender, green sprouts that grow after the rains. Their strong teeth snip off the dry, old stalks too. The coarse dried grass—called thatch—can also provide food nutrients. When zebra herds eat the thatch, they expose the tender, new grass below. Herds of wildebeests and gazelles graze among the zebras. They depend on the zebras to make the green grass available to them too. There's safety in being with so many other animals. More animals can watch for approaching predators.

The days pass calmly as the herds graze and slowly migrate north. The little male, almost three months old, spends almost as much time nibbling grass as nursing. He sometimes runs and plays with youngsters from neighboring zebra families. Once, when he's wandered a littler farther than usual, a cheetah slips up close. Most adults would be too big for this cat to hunt, but the little male is just the right size. Before the cheetah can attack, though, an alert stallion barks a warning. The little male flees to safety alongside the bigger adults.

The journey north continues.
When zebra stallions meet, they
pause long enough to sniff one
another from nose to rump. Then they walk on.
But the friendly exchanges stop immediately if a
stallion detects a scent telling him that a mare
is ready to mate. A young mare has recently
left her family group. One after another, the
stallions lift their head, roll back their
upper lips, and sniff her special scent.

Several fights break out among the stallions. While most of the stallions are distracted by the fighting, one bachelor stallion drives the mare away from the herd. Another stallion charges in to fight for her.

The mare trots away from the battle. The fighting stallions don't notice her. Snorting, with their ears laid back, they nip at one another's necks and faces. One chases the other into a water hole, and the battle becomes more intense. The stallions rear up, trying to bite whatever part of their rival they can reach.

Grunting, barking, and snorting, each stallion tries to bite his opponent's legs to cripple him. When this fails, one of the stallions turns quickly and kicks. The other stallion rears up just in time to avoid the deadly kick.

While the zebras watch the battling stallions, a pair of lionesses creep toward the herd. Suddenly, one of the big cats charges out of the tall grass. The zebras closest to the hunter squeal and thunder off. The little male runs so fast he's soon leading his family group. Panicked by the fleeing zebras, some of the wildebeests join the fleeing herd.

One lioness sees a mare that's lagging behind the escaping herd. In a burst of speed, the lioness grabs onto the zebra's hindquarters. The mare squeals in panic. The lioness digs in her claws. The zebra tries to run, but the effort of dragging the big cat slows her. Hanging on, the lioness sinks her teeth into her prey's belly. When the zebra collapses, the lioness quickly makes the kill.

Together the two lionesses eat the choicest parts of the zebra, including the juicy liver. They leave the rest to scavengers. Gliding on currents of warm air, a white-backed vulture is the first to spot the carcass on the ground. The bird circles to make sure the predators have gone. Then it lands, pokes its long neck into the zebra's open belly, and gulps down some of the flesh. As more vultures arrive, each newcomer jostles for a chance to feed. A black-backed jackal arrives and charges in to claim a share.

The scavengers leave only the bones. These become a meal for three hungry spotted hyenas. The zebra carcass has provided a meal for many different animals on the Serengeti Plain.

Meanwhile, the battle to claim the mare starts up again. When it's over, the mare becomes the newest member of the little male's family group. Life for the zebra herd goes back to its routine of walking and grazing. The constant search for fresh grass draws the grazers farther north. With each passing week, the little male grows bigger and stronger. Eventually, many zebras arrive at the banks of the Mara River. The animals push forward until those standing on the shore are forced into the water. Then they begin swimming across.

A big male crocodile glides toward the swimming zebras. Suddenly, the predator lunges, snapping its powerful big jaws onto a young stallion's belly. The crocodile pulls the zebra underwater to make the kill.

Other crocodiles attack the swimming zebras. One crocodile swims toward the little male and his mother. The mare bounds out of the water and runs back up the bank. The little male follows, leaping ashore just in time. The crocodile surges forward. Digging into the ground with his long claws, he follows the zebras onto the riverbank. But zebras can run faster on land than crocodiles. Even though he's smaller than this predator, the little male zebra has the advantage and escapes.

When he's a little more than a year old, the young male joins a group of other young stallions. He learns how to compete for a mate through play battles, which end before either stallion is injured. Then when he's three, the young stallion fights a fierce battle for a mare and wins.

The young stallion has started his own family group. With the birth of his mare's first foal, the cycle of life continues—a constant struggle to survive between predators and prey.

Looking Back

- Take another look at pages 12 and 13. Look at what features the predator has for attacking its prey. And think about the prey's defensive features. To find out more about this predator, read *Lions,* Animal Predators Series (Lerner Publications Company).

- Look at the zebras grazing on page 6 and drinking on page 17. See how the zebras' eyes are far above the mouth. How does that help the animals stay safe?

- Look in a book or check online to find a picture of a horse. Then compare the horse to the zebras pictured in this book. In what ways does a zebra look like a horse? Other than its stripes, in what ways does a zebra look different?

Glossary

BACHELOR: a mature stallion that has not yet established a family of breeding mares and their foals

FOAL: a baby zebra

HERD: a group of zebras

HOOF: a hard covering on the zebra's foot for protection when walking

MARE: a mature female zebra

MIGRATE: to move by season from one location to another for food and water

PREDATOR: an animal that hunts and eats other animals in order to survive

PREY: an animal that a predator catches to eat

SCAVENGER: an animal that feeds on dead animals, including prey killed by a predator

STALLION: a mature male zebra

STOMACH: the body part where chewed food begins to digest

More Information

BOOKS
Denis-Huot, Christine, and Michel Denis-Huot. *The Zebra: Striped Horse.* Watertown, MA: Charlesbridge Publishing, 1999. Photos and text show the lives of zebras in their natural habitat along with efforts to protect zebras and other members of the horse family.

Scuro, Vincent. *Wonders of Zebras.* New York: Dodd Mead, 1983. Investigate the evolution of zebras, their physical characteristics, and the efforts to help them survive.

Wexo, John Bonnett. *Zebra.* Poway, CA: Wildlife Education, 1999. Discover fascinating facts about zebras and their habitat.

VIDEOS
Families in the Wild-Zebras (Goldhill Home Media 2, 2001). Watch a zebra herd migrate in search of grass.

National Geographic Video: African Wildlife (Columbia Tristar, 1995). Witness a zebra mare defending her foal from a cheetah.

WEBSITES
Born to Roam
http://magma.nationalgeographic.com/ngm/0309/feature2/index.html?fs=www7.nationalgeographic.com
Two National Geographic photographers investigate the zebras roaming East Africa's plains.

Herds of Information
http://alumnus.caltech.edu/~kantner/zebras/
Find out about different kinds of zebras.

Index

With love for my son Scott and his wife, Heather, as they start their life together

The author would like to thank the following people for sharing their expertise and enthusiasm: Dr. Daniel Rubenstein, Chairman, Ecology and Evolutionary Biology Department, Princeton University, and Principal Investor of the Flagship Zebra Study, sponsored by a research grant from the National Science Foundation; Dr. Sue McDonnell, Head Equine Behavior Lab, University of Pennsylvania School of Veterinary Medicine; and Dr. John Fryxell, Zoology Department, specializing in behavioral ecology, University of Guelph, Canada. The author would also like to express a special thank-you to Skip Jeffery for his help and support during the creative process.

Photo Acknowledgments
© John Conrad/CORBIS, p. 1; © Anup Shah/naturepl.com, pp. 3, 5, 6, 15, 16, 18, 21, 27, 32, 36; © Stephen Frink/CORBIS, p. 7; © Alissa Crandall/CORBIS, p. 8; © Joe McDonald/CORBIS, p. 9; © A&M Shah/Animals Animals, pp. 10, 35; © Gallo Images/CORBIS, p. 11; © Tom Brakefield/CORBIS, pp. 12, 13, 29; © Richard Du Toit/naturepl.com, p. 14; © Art Wolfe/ArtWolfe.com, p. 17; © Tony Heald/naturepl.com, pp. 22, 31; © Gerald Hinde/ABPL/Animals Animals, p. 23; © Martin Harvey; Gallo Images/CORBIS, p. 25; © T.J. Rich/naturepl.com, p. 33; © Clem Haagner; Gallo Images/CORBIS, p. 37.
Cover: © Ami Vitale/Getty Images.

Copyright © 2007 by Sandra Markle

All rights reserved. International copyright secured. No part of this book may be reproduced, stored in a retrieval system, or transmitted in any form or by any means—electronic, mechanical, photocopying, recording, or otherwise—without the prior written permission of Lerner Publishing Group, except for brief quotations in an acknowledged review.

Lerner Publications Company
A division of Lerner Publishing Group
241 First Avenue North
Minneapolis, MN 55401 U.S.A.

Website address: www.lernerbooks.com

Library of Congress Cataloging-in-Publication Data

Markle, Sandra.
    Zebras / by Sandra Markle.
        p.   cm. — (Animal prey)
    Includes bibliographical references (p.   ) and index.
    ISBN-13: 978—0—8225—6062—3 (lib. bdg. : alk. paper)
    ISBN-10: 0—8225—6062—3 (lib. bdg. : alk. paper) 1. Zebras—Juvenile literature. I. Title. II. Series: Markle, Sandra. Animal prey.
QL737.U62M373 2007
599.665'7—dc22   2005036483

Manufactured in the United States of America
1 2 3 4 5 6 — DP — 12 11 10 09 08 07

ISAAC FOX LIBRARY